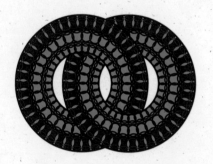

DARKENING
THE GRASS

MICHAEL
MILLER

DARKENING
THE GRASS

CavanKerry ◊ Press LTD.

CavanKerry Press Ltd.
Fort Lee, New Jersey
www.cavankerrypress.org

Library of Congress Cataloging-in-Publication Data

Miller, Michael, 1940-
Darkening the grass / Michael Miller. -- 1st ed.
    p. cm.
ISBN 978-1-933880-32-7 (alk. paper) -- ISBN 1-933880-32-5 (alk. paper)
I. Title.

PS3613.I5455D37 2012
811'.6--dc23

2012006312

Cover photograph by Mary Miller
Cover and interior design by Gregory Smith
First Edition 2012, Printed in the United States of America

CavanKerry Press is dedicated to springboarding the careers of previously unpublished, early, and mid-career poets by bringing to print two to three Emerging Voices annually. Manuscripts are selected from open submission; Cavankerry Press does not conduct competitions.

CavanKerry Press is grateful for the support it receives from the New Jersey State Council on the Arts.

Other Books by Michael Miller

The Joyful Dark (2008)

The Singing Inside (2011)

For William Leo Coakley

and to the memory of Robin Prising

CONTENTS

DARKENING
THE GRASS

I

WAITING

In the darkness before dawn
I open the window to smell a freshness
Sweeping up from the meadow
As the wind is waking.
Before arranging my rainbow of pills
Upon the table, I go into
This cool September day,
Walking down Heatherstone Road
Past cedars, pin oaks, spruces
And onto the meadow
Where the tall grass bends like the backs
Of women working in a field.
Milkweed leans in the breeze,
Wildflowers are closed,
And I sense something
In the distance, alive, watching me.
I pause and stare; he is there:
The young figure of the man I was.
He did not think of death.
Through a procession of years
He had never loved a woman.
He is looking at me,
Stooped, thin, white-haired man
With a white-stubbled jaw
In this meadow before
The sky splinters into light.
I stand before him,
I open my arms and draw him in
And remember the purity of
His loneliness in the midnight city
Dreaming of the woman he would meet,

The woman who would say his name
And calm his hunger.
I want to tell him: *Be patient,*
She is there, waiting.

COBRA

Each night you sigh
"Not today," then turn off
The bedside lamp, relieved
That a bomb did not explode
In the city where our son
Is still safe.
Terror nests in you.
We grow older,
Our son grows older,
But the terror doesn't change;
It rises in the dark,
Cobra-headed, rearing
Above everything you plant—
Roses, lilies, irises,
Its eyes yellow diamonds
Refracting all our deaths.

THE SWIMMER

You begin each day leaving our bed,
Going out into earth-scented air,
Crossing the grass to swim in the pond
Surrounded by a fence of cattails.
You have to swim each morning,
Peeling the dark,
Stripping the layers of memory
That bring you back to that night
In your top floor apartment
With a fire escape.
He struck you. His moonlit body
Covered you. His hand gripped a knife
And his palm pressed on the mattress
As he worked himself into you.
You prayed to live.
He stopped, gave up and left,
Slinking out the opened window
Through which he'd come,
Over rooftops, extending
The boundaries of violence.
You showered, trying to scrub him away,
Bathing three, four times a day.
And now you swim every morning,
Your strokes cutting through the surface
Of clear water, the spring-fed pond
That he can never reach.

ON THE SUNLIT FIELD

Like a sail in the windswept air
The one raised wing
Caught our eyes as we walked
Upon the sunlit field
And saw this bird,
A headless eagle
With that one raised wing,
A gravestone now,
Beside the bullet shells
Darkening the grass.

CUTTING AN ORANGE

Each morning I cut an orange into halves
And the halves into quarters, trying to make
Each segment equal, cutting evenly, precisely,
Beginning the day with this small claim
To order. You turn from a dream
At the noise I make in the kitchen.
Valencia, Seville, I whisper,
As though we were making love,
Then place the wedges on a plate,
This orange which has been picked
In Florida, then shipped north
And unpacked by alien hands.
If I can love this orange, what heights,
What horizons can I aspire to?
Can we eat it together,
Facing each other in Massachusetts
With nothing else between us?

INTO LIGHT

Morning, and the body unfolds
Before the tulips in the garden open
As the sun edges over the mountain
Where the hawk glides,
A kite without string.
Now I awaken to light
Yawning through the window,
To sleeves of the sun
Stretching out to us,
To the calls of cardinals
With crests of flame
And mourning doves wooing
The winter from my bones.
I turn from the blur of years
To nuzzle into your sleeping valleys
Before you move from loveliness
To rituals as the day arrives
Without mistakes or lies,
Without the frayed ends
Of old dreams or the loose ends
Of thoughts waiting to be tied.
Our bodies ease into openness
Like morning glories climbing
The trellis behind the house
While the remains of night disappear
Like stars in a constellation
We can only remember,
And then we consider
The divisions we live with,
The distance between
The soul's requirements

And the other life
That the day demands.
There are no beginnings or endings
But only the love which
Continues because it does,
Because it falls with
The last snow of winter
And rises with the tulips
That push into light.

II

EACH DAY

I

Sitting in the shadow
Of a rotting sycamore
He offends death,
Eating red meat, butter,
Welcoming each day,
This ninety-year-old man
Who fought in three wars,
Married twice, fathered
Seven, and dismisses
His doctor's advice.
In my sixty-seventh year
I listen to each word
Old Bill offers, marveling
At his stubborn will,
His desire to outlive
The sycamore.

II

Each day he gets dressed more slowly,
Sitting on the bed's edge
To lift his legs and push them
Through the dark tunnels
Of his frayed trousers
Where time works
Its steady disintegration.
No longer can he bend
Far enough to cut
His yellowed toenails that
Wear holes into his socks.
But he goes on, dressing
With determination, pleased
With this first accomplishment
Of the new day.

III

He looks at the raspberry pancake,
Thinks of blood clots,
Imagines death at breakfast,
And when his wife passes
The syrup he wants to grasp
Her hand around the bottle
And never let it go.
But he takes the syrup, pours it,
And swallows his fear
With each sweet bite.

IV

Shuffling across the porch,
He glances at the first snowdrops
That hang like pearls,
Pauses to light a cigarette.
Inhaling slowly, he is beyond
The arguments of his wife.
Old diehard, recalcitrant,
Nodding but not listening.

V

Lugging one leg after the other
Up the porch steps,
He settles into his chair
And finds pure pleasure
In the purple finches
That alight upon the feeder,
Watching their wings flutter
In the heaviness of the air.
Comfortable at last,
He needs nothing except
The company of birds.

VI

When the white tongues
Of waves licked his feet
Old Bill wished that
He could live by the sea,
Never leave his son's house.
But this son, his eldest,
Unsettles his soul;
Tension always sizzles
Like a fuse between them—
Alert, wary,
They can never love
Without an edge.

VII

He surrenders to stillness,
Closes his eyes,
Slows his breathing
And rehearses his death.
His wife comes onto the porch,
Puts her arms around his waist,
And kisses him lightly,
A soft feather of life.

VIII

When they arrive at the feeder,
Fluttering in the still air,
He tries to sing as beautifully
As he can to the cedar waxwings
With silvery gray feathers
And yellow-tipped tails.
They pay no attention
To the songs which draw him
Out of his shrunken body
And allow him to feel,
Momentarily, so happy.

IX

From the porch he watches a cat
Ready to spring at a small,
Yellow bird eating berries
Like drops of blood.
He wants to shout, to startle
The cat, warn the bird,
But remains silent,
Waiting for the teeth
To sink into feathers.
When it's over, the cat turns
With a mouthful of crushed gold
To stare at him, briefly,
Before leaving with its
Red-stained quarry.

X

Death looms like a storm cloud
But he refuses it,
Dwells only on the dragonfly
With transparent wings
Alighting on the lily,
On the love he feels
For every living thing,
Even the mosquito
Which lands upon his arm
That he gently blows away.

XI

Night: summer, humidity,
The porch light out,
Fireflies like dancers
Illuminating a dark stage
While Bill, rocking slowly,
Gazes at the lawn, wondering
If grass grows in the dark,
If worms lodge in
A dead man's bones.
These thoughts grow like weeds,
Wild, undisciplined in
The garden of his fears.

XII

If his wife dies first,
If his children abandon him,
If he is to be dragged
Through his remaining days
In a nursing home
Like a fish on a hook,
Old Bill will swallow
The pills he hoards
With a life-emptying act
Entirely his own.

XIII

He wishes he could ease upon her
Like mist covering a field at dawn
But his body is brittle
And moves without grace.
Yet when he lies beside her,
When he lifts a quavering hand,
His crooked fingers move
With a tenderness beyond age,
Beyond the light fading outside
Their window as they lie together,
Peacefully, in the late afternoon
Before the unsettling night.
If only they could die now,
If only their lives would close
Like the petals of an old rose!

III

YOUNG MARINES

He sat in Heaven's reading room
And in the dream, when I entered,
He looked up; we gazed at each other
Locking out the decades
Of separation and bringing back
Our eighteenth summer when we shared
The friendship of our lives.
Impassioned with life, vibrant
With ideas, braving any challenge,
We loved each other,
Young marines training for war.
We lusted, whoring after vision
Through the neon nights of Tijuana,
Driving back to Barstow through
The desert dawn as the sun rose
Like a gold medal, and we read
Hemingway, gatherers of his words
We hoped would inspire our own.
My friend advanced ahead of me
On a jungle trail where leaves hid
Trip-wires, spider webs for the wary.
An instant later I picked limbs
Out of the trees and placed them in
A body bag that I am still carrying.

SCARS

When I pass them in the forgiving field
A woman with a face as brown as earth smiles
And I see the scar across her forehead
And wonder if she was struck by shrapnel
In the rice paddies of Vietnam
Where she and the other women lived
Before they found sanctuary between
These hills in Massachusetts.
They work twenty acres
Without planes dropping napalm
Or rifles stuttering
From the tapestry of trees.
They always wave to me
And probably never consider
How I once carried a rifle
Through the jungles of their country.
I would like to take off my shirt
And show them the scar
On my back, then join them in the field
To work under the sun
In the slow dance of the wind.

LISTENING AT THE VFW

Time has creased his face,
Whitened his flat-topped hair
And stripped his words to truth.
He rolls up his sleeve,
Challenges a man
Half his age to arm wrestle.
Between shots of bourbon
At the corner table with
His back always to the wall,
He speaks of Iwo Jima,
Of the men he led up Suribachi,
And I commemorate
His eighty-fifth year
With a lifted glass,
Afraid to tell him
Anything, knowing
He has heard it all.

PRIVATE FIRST CLASS LAWLER

The sand clots his blood,
The desert clings to his soul,
And there is nothing
He can do to change it.
Timeless as its Tigris,
This Iraq is thick-skinned,
Like its water buffalos.
Mosul, Falluja, Baghdad,
This is where car bombs explode,
Here a suicide bomber presses
A button in the Ashur Street Market.
He was sent to Ramadi
From Wilmington, Vermont,
And here a sniper
Is looking for him.

PRIVATE COSTA

He kneels on the sand,
Riveted to the life
Flowing out of his friend,
The chunk of shrapnel
Jutting from his head.
He wants to scream, to cry,
But there is nothing
He can do, nothing he
Can say until he whispers
"I love you, I love you."
The words sound strange
Addressed to a man,
And he repeats them
As if to test their truth,
Then bends and kisses him,
Watching the blood
Sink into sand.

SERGEANT REESE

Despite the deaths in the desert,
The explosions in the shuddering air,
Despite watching the corpsman
With blue latex gloves
Picking up body pieces
And carrying them to a body bag
Like a dark cocoon on the sand,
Despite the sniper sneaking behind
The black robes on a clothesline
Across a flat rooftop in Sadr City,
Despite each mission at midnight
With his rifle pointing through
The green world of night vision goggles
As he hunts for insurgents with bullets
Waiting in dark chambers of their eyes,
Despite all this he can still dream of
Fly-fishing at sunrise, the Swift River
A blue road bending between towers
Of pine and hemlock and his yellow line
Whistling through the peaceful air.

HM1 MARTINEZ

He works to stop the bleeds,
To block off blood vessels
In the gaping hole in a groin,
To clog the sucking chest wound
With sterile gauze,
To push a combi-tube airway
Into a throat, to find
The bleeds and pack them,
To stabilize the bodies
And leave the dying,
To hurry to the next marine
He might be able to save.
"Hold the wound, pressure, pressure,"
A steady voice inside him urges
Between the groans, the cries,
The screams for morphine that
Will ricochet in his dreams
As guilt over the dead
Tears his soul like shrapnel,
Like bullets, blind and deadly.

CORPORAL RUSSELL

There are no mirrors in his room.
Five surgeries have begun
To restore his shrapnelled face,
This map of grafted skin,
This other face of war.
Once this face was handsome
That was kissed by women, looked upon.
You there, will you visit him?
On Sunday you will find him here.
No counseling, no surgery that day.
Let him say you are his friend.
He will close the blinds,
Turn off the light, and you
Can speak, you can listen to
His voice that has not changed.

LIEUTENANT DEMPSEY

He looks at his sleeping wife,
Her softness a cushion for the breeze
Coming through their window.
There is no rifle beside their bed,
A sniper is not on the next roof,
No bomb has been planted
In the road outside their house.
The view from their window
Offers no women in tangerine robes,
No merchants taking goods to a market.
He is not in Iraq,
He is waking in New Hampshire.
Now rise, lieutenant,
Pretend you have left it behind,
Pretend it will not affect
How you live this day,
That the call of the blue jay
Perched on a pine branch
Will not remind you
Of an incoming mortar
Before it explodes.

AFTER THE WAR

His dead days are done,
Buried away
From this beginning,
And he prays like a man
Who has left
A doorway of dark
That it will always be
This way.

Her hand strokes
His stump
Which feels like
The smooth top of
The Louisville Slugger
He swung as a boy
On the hot fields of
Greenville, Tennessee.

In the desert dust
After the bomb
The sickle of shrapnel
Cut through him,
What remains is what
Is left of his leg.

She never knew him whole.
They met after the gurneys,
The wheelchairs
Rolling down corridors
And lights like moons
In each room of doctors,
After the women who waited
Left him alone with their tears.

She did not weep or leave.
She fits him almost perfectly
Like his prosthesis.
Who cares why they love.
He has learned to love
His leg by watching her,
As if she were
An extension of it.

She is his complement,
His relief from his rage,
And he is the wound
She always wanted to heal,
The survivor who limps
Away from the wreckage
Into her arms again.

THE OLD VETERAN

Strapped down for safety
And breathing through a tube,
He hammered down the darkness.
Eighty years held up
His hawk-shaped head,
His sight was stronger
Than his tears,
His silence greater
Than every curse.
Steady before the strike,
His shaven chest
An empty shell,
His body fought
The waste of words,
Silence delivered
Each short breath.
Staring past the present,
Beyond the faceless crab
Crawling across his chest,
He turned from life
To leap at death,
A raging man spun
From the sun's hot scales.

IV

NOTHING UNDONE

Heart valves leak, blood pressure
Climbs its invisible ladder
Inside the arterial walls,
But he hopes to live past eighty,
An age that befriends the soul,
Outlives the invasion of fear.
He talks with his wife—
"What will you do, will you
Still live here?" He updates
His will, catalogs valuable books,
Leaves nothing undone
And resumes his routines,
Finding one specific pleasure
Within each ephemeral day.

MOVING

Each time he moved
He was afraid.
His books stacked in boxes
Seemed like his body
Packed in its coffin.
Moving, he knew, was part
Of a cycle, a change
To sharpen his senses.
Still he dreaded it.
He wanted everything
To remain as it was:
The same rooms, routines,
The same people to greet.
He needed to keep the illusion
That if he never moved
He wouldn't be an inch closer
To the next landlord, death.

THE RESULTS

Will the white cells devour the red,
Will his doctor speak death
In his clear voice?
Like this morning's bitter coffee
He can almost taste his death.
He wants to believe
He no longer cares
Whether he lives or dies,
Whether his wife's love
Will be wedded to sorrow
And his son's tears
Disguised by a smile.
In his seventy-fifth year
His small, individual life
Has no more significance
Than the nebulous stars.
His final choice will be
Whether to die
In an unrestful hospital room
Or whether to lift the pistol
From beneath the shirts in his drawer,
Place it against his temple
And squeeze.
Either way, he will finally
Be done with it.
There will be no more precautions
To take, no more illusions of safety.
There will be nothing left for him to do.

HUNGER

Will he welcome the emptiness of death,
The relief from his anticipation,
Or will it come like an obscene guest
He cannot turn away? Wondering is better
Than the locked doors, the drawn shades,
The absence of tumultuous life.
He has always been insatiable,
Wanting to swallow the sunrise,
Not compromise, not sacrifice
The hungers eating away his conflicting selves.
Is it possible that finally,
In the deep December of his eighth decade,
He is hungering for death,
Wanting to chew it slowly, day by day?
He knows its omnipresence,
Its sweetness, its bitterness, its aftertaste.
He will fatten on death.

THE WOLF

I

What waits in darkness,
In the hours of the wolf?
He closes his eyes,
Thinks of the night
His son was born,
His small head a pink,
Wet bulb emerging,
The midwife cutting
The umbilical cord—
Lifting him into light.

II

A blind eye in the black face
Of the sky shines through
His window, drawing him
Toward death's empty desert
And the silence of the wolf
That will lie upon his chest,
Peering into his eyes.

III

He bolts awake with fear,
With sweat blistering his forehead,
With dread of the scalpel

Opening his chest,
The surgeon entering his heart
That has been loving,
Cruel, indifferent.

IV

The wolf sits on his bed,
Its eyes reveal nothing
Of truth, of lies,
And he watches it draw closer,
Smells its breath of ashes
And clover, hears its heart
Drumming his name.

V

He shivers through the cold
And pretends the woolen blankets
Are a body covering him,
Pretends that a woman
Is lying upon him, taking
His terror into her lair.

VI

Only for a minute does it last,
The erection he awakens with,
Touches, imagining his crooked
Fingers straightening,
Old body changing, skin,
Wrinkled, becoming taut,
Youth restored.

VII

Are those two pale stars
The eyes of the wolf
Gazing down at him?
They fade into first light
As he rises with
The whisper of daybreak
Drawing him out of his bed.

VIII

He walks beneath trees,
Their leaves tilting with light.
Wherever the wolf has gone,
Outcast, cut off
From all things human,
 It waits for the dark to return.

V

THE ALIEN BEGINS HIS DAY

Each morning he rises with his alien eyes
Peering through the walls of the dark.
The alarm goes off, the news begins,
And he walks toward the dresser,
Toward the long-stemmed lily still climbing
Its invisible ladder of light.
Each morning he puts on a monogrammed shirt
As soft as the skin of the woman stirring in bed
Who said his name over brandy, by the fire,
After Beethoven, or when her body revealed
Its moles like points on a map, setting off
The fairness of skin, and when he hears his name
With its syllables leading him down a stairway
Of sound, the meaning of it leaves him as quickly
As the spider who crawls beneath the sink
When he washes the night from his face.
It was a night which explained nothing at all,
Not why he awakened, not why his brain
Has forgotten his dream of a woman dressed
In a map of Brazil, of a boy crossing plantations
With snakes, tarantulas, and horses grazing in
The shadow of mountains he climbed in his sleep,
Not why his body feels like a cord of muscle
Stretching with pain, not why his red-rimmed eyes
Blink messages of mortality to the face in the mirror
Or why his tongue feels like an old dry sponge.

When he finishes breakfast, when he looks
At the crumbs and leftover crusts, he thinks of
Body bags lined on a tarmac and waiting for transport,
Of uniforms pressed with medals of blood.

Then he goes out, he opens the door
Where a handful of moths cling to the screen
As if they were waiting for signals of light,
And he listens, he listens for the first bird
To call from the highest branch of the blue spruce
And wants to know why its song is without meaning to him,
Why its shrill tone neither trumpets the sun
Nor his setting forth in the silver Mercedes.
He has listened carefully through a lifetime
Of rituals and disciplines, attentive to prescriptions
Of the air, warnings in the wind, but he has learned
Nothing except that the bird sings only because it must
Just as he must begin again trying to escape
The white cage of his bones, must fit his hand
Into the woman's hand as if it were a glove cut
From the leather of his soul, must move his cheek
Against the hollow in her face and touch death
For a moment, must question what his cigars
And mistresses have amounted to in the equation
Of his life before it is erased from a blackboard
Of the night, must question the reasons
For traveling which unsettles his thoughts.

He returns to the quest for significance
In the continual journey which turns in his mind
Like the cards in an old woman's hand
Who plays at the table with strangers and friends
Dressed in the light, who made the choices
Of blouses or shirts, butter or jam,
Who decided upon the bus or the train,
Who have begun their day as he has begun his,
With the alarm going off, with the news coming on,
With bombings and murders with his coffee and toast
And obituaries exact as a grocery list.
He hides his forgetfulness and pain

With a habitual smile, a diffident greeting,
An unmindful exchange about the weather,
The weekend, the trip to Caracas and the death
Of a senator, about anything except the estrangement
That gnaws at his heart and congeals his blood,
The estrangement he feels from his wife
Who plants her sorrow with seeds in the garden,
The estrangement he feels from his son
Who tattoos his arms with his dreams,
While all the time he needs to draw closer,
To begin each day with the tentative
Fumbling efforts rooted in shyness and shame
That will bring him closer to love,
To all that appears alien, like the bones
In the earth, like the fugitive notes
Of the full-hearted bird beginning to sing.

VI

NO AGENDA

Through the summer's thick darkness
He hears the birds' call, "Get up, get up,"
And he rises expectantly because
He is alive in his ninth decade.
Now he can walk leisurely,
Listen to the black-masked cardinal,
Look closely at the clusters of lilies
Unfolding like tongues of gold.
Once he would have driven quickly by,
Beginning his long day's agenda,
But now he heeds the birds' call
And begins each day without a plan.

MOWING

Back and forth he walks across
The lawn in lines unwavering
And when the soft green splinters
Fly into the summer-laden air
He feels a freedom
Unrestricted as the sun
While meadowlarks and sonnets
Sing inside his head,
Leavening his heart with
Gratitude for grass to cut.

WILDWOOD CEMETERY

Each dawn he walks where sleepers never waken
And when he sees a fox like a streak of flame
Flashing across the grass oblivious to
The gravestones or a file of turkeys strutting
Through a doorway of leaves or a raccoon
Waddling like an old man with heavy pockets,
The dread of death he carries like a tarnished coin
Vanishes as a goldfinch rises toward the sky.

FLIGHT

He stands at sunrise on his snowy field—
Too soon for birds, but he imagines them:
The fork-tailed swallows, scarlet tanagers,
Yellow-throated warblers, then his wife with
Wings, her long white body lifting from
A sunlit pond and gliding toward him.
He wishes he could be a bird
Flying beside her, leaving their
Aging bodies and the shortening days.
He would like them to die together,
Pressed close, like feathers.

AN OLD COUPLE

His stomach, a sagging moon,
Reminds him of his pregnant wife
Fifty years ago, this woman
Wrinkled into wisdom
Who sleeps beside him.
Lifting his arthritic legs,
He looks down and smiles;
His pectorals hang like breasts
With nipples lounging in the dark.
Old and together, he thinks,
With children gone and dreams
Sent out like letters
To a wrong address.
Now there is this: the coffee
To make, the newspaper to read,
And tulips to be picked
And savored for their
Short-lived tenure.

MARRIAGE

There might be a thousand leaves
On this massive ginkgo tree,
Each shaped like a small fan
That would cool her on
This sultry summer day,
Just as in winter when she shivers
He warms her with each
Essential part of him.

WALKING

When he stands in one place
For longer than a minute
His old knees feel like
Eggshells cracking slowly,
And so he walks, determined
To outdistance death.
He walks toward the thrush
Singing on a branch,
The roses with petals
Like opened lips,
And always toward his wife
Who is walking in her garden
Where she, too, feels death
Trailing steadily behind
The blue irises.

THE FLOWERS

Now he is too ill to walk
To the window and see her garden,
A dazzle of flowers brightening
Their front yard, the lilies
Like trumpets pointing toward the sun,
The irises like twists of sea and sky,
All blossoming from bulbs and seeds
Without haste or delay,
Without knowledge of the bloom to come
Or the stark, inevitable decline.
She brings him cut flowers,
Arranges them in a vase beside his bed,
Then kisses him lightly, lightly
As a butterfly upon his lips.

ACKNOWLEDGMENTS

The following poems, some in slightly different versions, have been previously published:

Chariton Review: "Into Light"
Chautauqua Literary Journal: "Cutting an Orange"
Commonweal: "On the Sunlit Field"
Hanging Loose: "Private First Class Lawler"
Mudfish: "The Swimmer"
New York Quarterly: "Young Marines," "Listening at the VFW," "Lieutenant Dempsey"
Nimrod International Journal: "Marriage"
North American Review: "Private Costa"
Ontario Review: "The Alien Begins His Day"

Poet Lore: "Cobra"

Poetry East: "Mowing"

Raritan: "Sergeant Reese"

Rattle: "Corporal Russell"

Sanctuary: "Wildwood Cemetery"

Sow's Ear Poetry Review: "Flight"

Witness: "Scars"

"Each Day" was published as a limited edition chapbook by Adastra Press.

"The Old Veteran" appeared in *Jackhammer*, a limited edition published by Helikon Press.

CAVANKERRY'S MISSION

Through publishing and programming, CavanKerry Press connects communities of writers with communities of readers. We publish poetry that reaches from the page to include the reader, by the finest new and established contemporary writers. Our programming brings our books and our poets to people where they live, cultivating new audiences and nourishing established ones.

OTHER BOOKS IN THE EMERGING VOICES SERIES

The display type for this book is set in Bodoni, an
18th-century typeface designed by Gianbattista Bodoni.
The Bodoni font is notable for the great contrast between
its thin and thick strokes. The book's text was set in New
Caledonia, a 1980s variation of the Caledonia typeface
originally designed for Linotype by William Addison
Dwiggins in 1938.